He Touched Her

BY ELEANOR W. CUNNINGHAM
& DORIS M. McDOWELL

WARNER PRESS, INC.

Anderson, Indiana

He Touched Her
By Eleanor W. Cunningham and Doris M. McDowell

First Published by Warner Press
Anderson, Indiana

On-Demand Reprint Edition

Perfect Bound
ISBN 978-1-60416-495-4 Item #01111

Reformation Publishers
242 University Drive
Prestonsburg, Kentucky 41653
www.reformationpublishers.com
rpublisher@aol.com
Fax 606-886-8222
1-800-765-2464
606-886-7222

Printed and bound in the United States of America

Dedicated to the memory of
Anne's father
C. Albert Eklund

Preface

In reading this record of Anne Wetzell's illness and healing one might be tempted to categorize these events as merely unusual and Anne herself as being lucky. Although Anne's illness, post transfusion thrombocytopenia, is uncommon we are challenged in this book to see beyond the illness itself. We are challenged to see a follower of Christ face illness with him.

God's Word answers two very difficult questions regarding affliction, who is responsible and why. Clearly, God is responsible for Moses' stuttering as God asks rhetorically, "Who makes mouths?" (Exodus 4:11). Secondly, in John 9:3, Jesus explains that the man born blind was able to demonstrate the power of God. Illness, like life, in its proper perspective points to God. As a physician involved in the treatment of children with blood diseases, God's Word challenges me to see beyond the immediate suffering, to seek understanding, and to praise him for being in charge of the past, present, and future. Of the ten lepers healed by Jesus only one returned to praise God and thus receive spiritual healing (Luke 17:17-19). This book, like the leper who returned, seeks to praise God for what He has done.

King David felt the hand of God on his son (2 Samuel 12:22). He realized that it was God's prerogative to be merciful and heal his son. David was drawn closer to God by this experience. Many times, despite our prayer, our laying on of hands, our good works, or our wills, the Angel of Death intrudes. We experience in some fraction the infinite grief and anguish which God experienced when his Son, Jesus Christ, became sin itself that we might through his innocent blood become the children of God. The Spirit of Truth inspired the Apostle Paul as a Hebrew-Christian to write, "Neither death, nor life, nor angels, nor principalities, nor powers, nor things present, nor things to come, nor height, nor depth, nor any other creature, shall be able to separate us from the love of God, which is in Christ Jesus our Lord" (Romans 8:38-39).

The Good Shepherd claims his sheep and regardless of illness or its outcome, his sheep belong to him for all eternity.

Frederick B. Ruymann M.D.
Wheaton, Maryland
August 23, 1972

Introduction

In May of 1971 Anne Wetzell of Rockville, Maryland should have died. Miraculously, she lived.

The doctors said Anne could not possibly live because she had lost so much blood from a rare condition that set in after a routine operation. The cause was a mystery that baffled them. Her life seeped away. Then God stepped in and touched her.

In this tremendous experience was demonstrated an extraordinary kind of love that drew together people in unusual places and under unusual circumstances. Out of it to Anne and her family came the realization that in the family of God are hundreds of people who pray, who believe, who are ready and willing to hold steady, to watch by the bedside and give of their blood in order that someone in dire need may truly live again.

Also into the lives of Anne and her family came a sequence of events that showed beyond a doubt that there is a Master Designer who plans for all those who put their trust in him. This plan he beautifully revealed as they prayed and followed the leadings of his Spirit and believed the promises of God's Word.

I first met Anne Wetzell in January 1971. We became Christian friends. Because of this association I was able to lend her my support and love and prayers while she went through this extraordinary experience. Although my sharing this event with Anne brought great burden to my heart, it also brought a tremendous peak of spiritual fulfillment as I saw God hear and answer prayer in a marvelous way.

Since God had performed so miraculously in the life of Anne and so many persons have been touched by it, the Lord seemed to direct me to put it in story form. It is my hope that it might be a blessing to all who read of God's gracious dealings in the life of one of his dear children.

I am very grateful to the following people who contributed generously and willingly of their experiences: Anne and Howard Wetzell, Diane Marie Wetzell, Myrtle Eklund, Connie Ekstrom, Kay Kramm, Reverend James B. Jones, Dorothea Webber, and Dr. Frederick B. Ruymann, M.D. Thanks also to my husband, Floyd E., and three children, Floyd T., Janice, and Diane whose patient understanding allowed me to spend so many hours apart from them.

I am also deeply grateful to my friend, Doris M. McDowell, who gave not only invaluable editorial assistance but also encouragement and inspiration, without which this book could not have been written.

Eleanor W. Cunningham

Contents

Chapter 1

Miracle Among Us

It was a hot Sunday morning in June 1971. The little white church on Brookes Avenue was nearly filled to capacity. The audience listened while the organ thrilled their minds and hearts in worshipful meditation. The service that day was much like other services had been until the young pastor said, "There is in our audience today a person who has recently experienced a miracle of healing. Just a few weeks ago she lay critically ill in George Washington University Hospital with a blood condition that threatened her life. What a joy it is to have Anne Wetzell with us today. Her presence alone is a testimony to God's power." Then, turning to her, he said, "Anne, would you like to give a word of testimony?"

Anne, an attractive woman with a radiant smile and twinkling blue eyes, rose to speak. Her words poured forth with all the gratitude of a loving, human heart.

"I praise the Lord for allowing me to live and for the privilege of being here today. It is only through the mercy of God that I am here, and I'm so grateful for the healing ministry of Christ, my Savior.

"I'm grateful, too, for friends who have prayed for me and I thank God for the love you have shown to me, along with the prayers, the flowers, the cards, and your life's blood you stood so ready to give."

So this is the story of that miracle.

Anne Marie Wetzell was born in Brockton, Massachusetts, an only child of Albert and Myrtle Eklund. Theirs was a Christian home, and Anne learned to love the Lord at an early age, making her commitment to Christ at the age of twelve.

She had the usual ups and downs of teen-agers during the formative years, but God was faithful and her desire to serve him became strengthened in the lessons he taught her.

Summers were spent at Cape Cod where Anne gathered little children about her to tell them Bible stories. Her day was not complete until they had come and she had shared some truth with them out of the Word of God.

Since serving others seemed to be the direction of the Lord for her life, when high school was finished Anne entered nurses' training. Of all the specialized fields, Anne loved working in the emergency room the most—things happened there, they needed her, and she could help those who were in desperate condition. It was an exciting place to be and full of drama.

But summer came and with it vacation at Buzzard's Bay. There she met a young, handsome graduate of the Merchant Marine Academy, Howard Wetzell, and Anne's nursing career came to an abrupt end.

They were married in 1954 in Brockton, Massachusetts and went to live in California, where Howard was to take special training for the Navy. Soon Diane Marie, a lovely daughter, was born.

From the beginning their lives were welded to the church and its activities, and God's hand began to move in these lives so committed to him.

But commitment often means change in our own plans. One morning Howard received the offer of a job with IBM in Owego, New York. But Anne said, "I don't want to move away from here. I like Boston, my friends, and my church." The thought that it just might be God leading them out had not entered her mind. But they made it a special matter of prayer. The answer came a few days later while they were at Word of Life Camp. Howard was on an errand for the camp. While he was gone Anne went to their room. There kneeling before the Lord she asked him to make her willing if it was his will for them to move.

It was Thursday. After Bible study they went to the dining hall for lunch where the hostess directed them to the table with an older couple, Theresa and Kenneth Kemp, who were already seated.

Getting acquainted with them, they learned that the Kemps lived in Endicott, New York (just a few miles from Owego), and that Mr. Kemp worked for IBM. It seemed the Lord had led them to the Kemps and during that lunchtime many questions were answered.

"One of my hang ups about moving to Owego was schooling for Diane," Anne said, "so I asked the Kemps about the schools." Kenneth said, "Well, I'm on the school board and things are going very well."

When they inquired about housing, he answered, "I'm on the town planning board; it's quite a progressive area."

At this point Anne could not keep the tears back. "They ran down my cheeks," she said, "and then I opened up my heart and told those puzzled new friends about our job offer that required a quick answer, and how I hadn't wanted Howard to accept it. Then I told them how I had prayed and how the Lord was using them to show us his leading.

"We left that lunch table rejoicing in the quiet peace the Lord had given, sure of his leading, happy to have met these new friends in Christ.

"We moved to Owego and enjoyed wonderful years of Christian growth in fellowship with a new pastor and new friends in a church in nearby Endwell. That friendship continues to last even though the Lord has directed us again into another field of service."

Chapter 2

Open Hearts and Open Doors

Anne and Howard were very happy and busy in their new church. There they immediately found numerous places to serve. Howard was elected Sunday school superintendent and also became the teacher of the young adult class. Anne helped in the nursery, conducted children's choir, and taught in vacation Bible school. The church was their life. Frequently they entertained church groups in their home where many found new life. They were happy and satisfied until a certain evangelist came to their church for a week of meetings.

On Friday night Harry Jueckstack brought a message about Christians in the institutional church who have no time to speak to their neighbors about Christ. "Day after day, week after week," he said, "Christians are so busy they do not reach out to the unchurched who need him." Anne listened, the Holy Spirit spoke, and at the close of the service she went forward to make a new commitment to the Lord. From now on she determined to have time for her neighbors. It was the beginning of a new pattern of life for her. How quickly the truth of the evangelist's words came to life as she prayed and looked for opportunities! God opened doors for her to witness. It was true! She found time to speak to all of her neighbors and to others to tell them what Christ meant to her and what he could also mean to them. She happily found that it was possible for her, a very busy church worker, to take the time to witness effectively and with results, something she had never dreamed possible.

It was early in 1968 when IBM transferred Howard to Maryland. After considerable house hunting in the suburbs of Washington, D.C., they settled in the Flower Valley subdivision of Rockville, about six miles from Howard's office in Gaithersburg. The events that followed again proved the providence of God had placed them there.

Among their new friends was Kay Kramm, a neighbor, who invited Anne to attend Christian Women's Club meetings in the area. Anne had been acquainted with this national organization before but only in a casual way. Learning of the way these Christian ladies shared their faith and personally ministered to those who needed Christ, Anne saw a way that she could put into action her new commitment to her Lord.

Their secret was in the morning "coffees" at which women informally gathered weekly or monthly to study the Word of God. There the unchurched but spiritually hungry women were introduced to Jesus Christ. The study was simple—direct but dynamic. Miracles were happening; lives were being changed. Women who would never think of going to church were opening both their homes and hearts to the gospel. And other women who had never dared be active in their own churches were finding themselves able to minister in a meaningful way to their own neighbors as study guides.

Here was an open door for Anne to follow. By nature a warm, friendly person with a spontaneous smile, she was able to put even a stranger at ease. This new association encouraged and developed the desire for sharing what God had put into her heart. From the life of this dedicated woman many sincere searchers after the Word of life heard the simple gospel message and felt the loving touch of a sincere Christian over a cup of coffee.

In 1969 Anne was elected to be the prayer group chairman of the Christian Women's Club for the Washington suburban area. In this capacity she helped organize prayer and Bible study groups. She conducts a most successful one in her own neighborhood and is often invited to begin new ones in new areas all because—He leads!

There in Flower Valley, a typical affluent suburban area, Anne found fulfillment sharing the love of Christ with others. It was a new and exciting way of life. Certainly God had enlarged her spiritual vision.

And then, suddenly, in May 1971 Anne was stricken with a rare physical malady and the vision faded. For days she lay there too sick to hope, too weak to pray! Howard would have to pray and hope for all of them—alone!

Chapter 3

The Nightmare Begins

On Saturday, May 15, 1971 the sun was shining and the multi-colored azaleas along George Washington Parkway were blooming in their splendor but Howard Wetzell didn't notice. Deep in his heart a battle raged between fear and faith. Anne lay dying and medically there was little hope of her recovery. The past week had been a nightmare that had grown worse as the days went by. Yet God's Word was true, and Howard's faith was in his promise. He knew God would not fail. But it would take a miracle, and for this Howard struggled to believe.

He turned off the Parkway onto Whitehurst Freeway, then right on twenty-second street and into the parking lot across from George Washington University Hospital. Mechanically he turned the car over to the parking lot attendant, quickly stepped across the street, ran up the concrete steps into the lobby, and hurried back to the elevators. As he pushed the "up" button he wondered what was waiting for him on the floor above.

Howard's appearance would not have revealed to the casual observer the turbulence within. He stood erect even now, his shoulders back, his chin up, his steady blue eyes looking straight ahead. Always calm, conservative, and quiet the nature of the man was not easily discernible from the outside. While Howard Wetzell always kept his emotions well controlled, those who knew him best found him to be extremely kind and sensitive especially toward those he loved.

Anne's room was No. 13025 at the end of the corridor. As Howard started in, Dr. Arnold Lear was coming out. Stopping Howard, he said, "Can you get ten people for blood donors for your wife?" Howard replied, "I can get more than ten people if you want them." The doctor said, "No, we just need ten pints of blood. We are going to operate today. The Red Cross is closed and we have to process the blood here. We have notified our lab technicians. Can you have the donors here by one o'clock?"

"Yes," Howard replied, trying to keep the fear out of his voice. "I think I can have them here by one."

Hurrying to the phone downstairs, he made three telephone calls. One was to Dr. Bill Culver in his office at IBM; one to his good friend, Jack Timmons, a neighbor in Flower Valley; and the other call was to Reverend Jim Jones, pastor of the Church of the Nazarene in Gaithersburg. He knew he could count on every one of them to come through for him. It is good to have friends who will stand by, thought Howard thankfully as he retraced his steps to the elevators.

Upstairs the nurses with hurried efficiency set about their tasks. They were unsmiling and serious. It seemed to Howard there was a heavy solemnity over the entire floor. That fear still gripped him making him feel ill. What if something happened to Anne? O God, be with her right now. Don't let anything happen to her. Please God. . . . He sat down in the little waiting room near the elevators where he had spent many hours that week. For the hundredth time his mind went back over the events of the past several days.

Anne had entered Columbia Hospital for Women in Washington, D.C. at the direction of her doctor, Dr. Thomas A. Wilson, gynecologist, on May 4. He was to perform a hysterectomy. However, tests in the hospital indicated Anne had a very low blood condition and before surgery could be performed the next day she would have to have two blood transfusions. These were administered that evening.

That night Anne was fitful and restless. She felt ill and had difficulty sleeping. Early the next morning Pastor Jones came in, as is his custom, to have prayer with her before the preoperative sedation. He prayed and read the Bible and stayed until she was wheeled into surgery. She seemed strengthened by the pastor's visit.

Upon waking from the operation Anne saw her good friend, Kay Kramm, waiting for her. (Howard had had to go to Syracuse unexpectedly on business, but he'd come the very minute he returned.) Kay's strong faith in God and confidence in his Word always gave Anne a feeling of security. Dr. Wilson came in shortly to reassure her. "The operation was successful, young lady, but the nurses will be giving you two more blood transfusions today. We want to be sure!" Anne liked

Dr. Wilson, and his kind, personable manner made her glad she was under his care.

After he'd gone, she closed her eyes and recalled how the Lord had directed her to the right Dr. Wilson when there were two by the same name in Washington. It was over—and Anne was confident she'd be all right.

She had been doctoring in Endwell, New York and was aware that sooner or later she would have to have this operation. Since she was new in the Washington area, she had inquired of a neighbor if she knew of a good gynecologist. She was very particular about who was to take care of her and had her own ideas about the type of doctor she wanted.

The friend knew a nurse in a local hospital. She called her and asked, "If you were going to have a hysterectomy, who would you have as your doctor?" The nurse immediately replied, "Dr. Thomas Wilson."

Anne prayed, "Lord, if this is not the doctor I should have, close the doors. Don't let him take me." She made an appointment. As she sat in the waiting room she prayed, "Lord, please give me some sign as to whether I will be satisfied with this doctor."

When she went into his office, the first thing he said was, "How did you happen to come to me?" Anne told him of the recommendation of the nurse. Then he said, "I don't know if you have the right Thomas Wilson. There are two of us, and both have the middle initial *A*. You have my permission to change if you want to." He told Anne that he was Assistant Chief of

Staff at Columbia Hospital for Women. That was enough; she was satisifed that this was the leading of the Lord!

Anne ate well, slept well, and entertained several visitors in the days following the operation with only the usual discomfort expected of this type of surgery. The phone by her bed rang almost constantly with interested friends inquiring about their beloved Anne.

On Monday, May 10, she learned she would be released from the hospital the following day. She looked forward to being home with her family and her mother, who had come on Mother's Day to spend a couple of weeks while Anne recuperated.

Monday for Howard was a routine day at the office, except that he told his boss he would be leaving early Tuesday to take Anne home. That afternoon he had a phone call. It was Anne. She was upset and crying and said she was "bleeding from her mouth." There was pleading in her voice when she said, "Can you come right away?" Of course he could. He quickly called Anne's mother, Mrs. Eklund, and told her he would pick her up in just a few minutes and they would go to the hospital together. She seemed a little surprised at his request that she go with him, but said she would hurry and get ready.

When Howard arrived home, Diane met him at the door. "What's wrong, daddy? I just talked to mommy on the phone and she was crying."

"Don't worry, honey," Howard said reassuringly as he pushed a strand of her long blond hair back over her shoulders, "I'm going to the hospital now. I'll call you and let you know how mommy is." Her eyes looked troubled as she waved to Howard and her grandmother as they pulled out of the driveway.

Howard could not help but be anxious as his mind tried to fathom what he had heard. "Anne told Diane on the phone that she had 'petechiae' all over . . . she said something about spots on her skin and that she was hemorrhaging!" Mrs. Eklund was worried! She searched Howard's face as they sped along to the hospital. "Howard, what do you make of it? Did you ever hear of anything like that?"

"I don't know, mother. It doesn't sound good. We'll soon find out." It was good to have Anne's mother to talk to. The years had stamped upon her countenance the marks of strong character and determined will, while her gentle eyes revealed kindness and understanding. She had always liked Howard and he knew it. Knowing she was a woman of great faith was reassuring to him right now. Even though they did not say it, each knew the other was praying.

When they walked into her room that Monday afternoon, they could see something was different about Anne. The night before she had been lively, cheerful, and eager to come home. Now she was very depressed, nervous, and upset. Anne had noticed the spots (hemorrhaging through the skin), and when Dr. Stewart Becker, the intern, came in she told him she felt sure that she knew what she had. The intern said he never had seen anything like this before.

"Oh, Howard, I'm so glad you've come." Her eyes showed her relief at his arriving so soon. "I'm so afraid. Look at me! I'm bleeding right through my skin. Before you came I took a big blood clot out of my mouth. I'm *so* tired. Something's wrong. Oh, Howard, mother, please pray."

Howard, outwardly calm, seated himself on the bed, taking Anne's hand in his. The sweet smell of the flowers in the room rather sickened him. He never had liked the combination of smells in hospitals and for that reason had stayed away from them whenever he could.

Mrs. Eklund drew up a chair near Anne's bed. "Now honey, tell us just what happened. You looked so good last night when we left."

"Well for one thing I didn't sleep too well. I guess I was excited about going home. Then this morning when I took a walk down the corridor I felt very tired and had a hard time getting back to my bed. I thought perhaps it was because I hadn't slept well. Some of my Bible study women with Dorothea Webber came in to see me. When they left I felt very peculiar. Something warm came in my mouth and I found it was a large blood clot. I was scared. When I looked at the rest of my body, I found these spots all over my skin. Quickly getting out of bed, I went to the mirror. When I looked at my mouth, I was also bleeding from my gums. Even my eyes are bloodshot. Desperately frightened now, I called Dr. Becker. 'Look at me, Doctor. I have petechiae.' He tried to relieve my fears, but Howard, I think it's getting worse. Can't you do something?"

When Howard talked with Dr. Becker, it was the same explanation he had given Anne—the stress of the operation and her low blood. But somehow what he said was not very convincing and Howard sensed that there had not been a satisfactory diagnosis of Anne's condition at this point. He and Mrs. Eklund stayed as long as they were permitted. About 7:30 they had prayer with Anne, committing her into the keeping of the One who knows all things.

Even with a sedative Anne had too much pain to sleep. Dr. Becker sat by her bed most of the night. He was good company, witty, cheerful, and sympathetic. It was good just to have him there. When Anne tried to pray, it was difficult, for the pain was increasing. Finally, weary, bewildered, very ill, she dozed a little and waited for the morning.

Chapter 4

Platelets and Prayer

Howard's mother had died from a blood problem and he knew Anne's condition could be just as serious. As he and Myrtle Eklund drove toward home that Monday evening, there were few words. Each was lost in thoughts of the bewildering events that had transpired that day. Each struggled to send faith and prayer up to God who was, and had always been, their refuge.

That evening when Pastor Jim Jones learned that Anne had taken a sudden turn for the worse he rushed to the hospital. He was greeted in the hall by Kay Kramm, Anne's close friend, who had been with her for just a few minutes. She told him that Anne's condition was very serious. She showed deep concern for her future. When they went back into the room Pastor Jones observed Anne's bloody mouth and the black and blue coloring on the exposed portions of her arms, her face, and her neck. He tried to speak reassuring words and prayed a short prayer. It was difficult for him to be his usual cheerful, optimistic self, however, for before him lay a sight such as he had never seen: a fellow-Christian facing a puzzling and terrifying setback.

Walking down the corridor after the visit, Kay and Pastor Jones discussed her condition. She could only surmise about the symptoms, but she felt the situation was indeed very unusual. Pastor Jones left the hospital very heavyhearted, caught in a spiral of gloom and disappointment that pulled his faith down and left him with a concern he could not shake off.

Tuesday morning Anne was no better. Dr. Wilson came in to see her and said he was going to call in a hematologist, a blood specialist. They knew Anne was reacting violently to something, but what they could not tell. Her platelet count, normally about 250,000, had gone down to below 10,000. The terrible pain in the incision was getting worse and she was hemorrhaging from it. Blood was also found in her kidneys.

When they began making so many tests, Anne feared she had a fatal blood disease. The doctor was to make a test that day, taking marrow from the bone, to determine if it was producing normally. Dr. Jack Reingold was called in to do the bone marrow biopsy, a very painful procedure.

In the afternoon when Howard came in, Anne poured out her fears to him, telling him about the biopsy. Standing by her bed, he held her hand and prayed that the biopsy would be favorable. What great relief and thankfulness filled their hearts when later the report came. The marrow was normal, ruling out Anne's fear of leukemia.

But Anne's condition worsened as the hours went by. Finally Mrs. Eklund said to Howard, "I believe we'd better let her father know about this. He is so close to Anne, and I don't see any improvement." Howard agreed, so Mrs. Eklund called, urgently advising him to come at once. Anne was worse and there were complications.

Albert Eklund, Anne's father, arrived about noon on Wednesday at National Airport in Washington. Howard spotted him coming toward them in the crowd of passengers. How much he looked like Anne—his round face, the clear blue eyes, and ready smile, even his way of walking. His hair was nearly white, a little thin on top, and it seemed to Howard that the droop of his shoulders was a little more pronounced than would have been caused by the one suitcase he was carrying.

The first thing he said to Myrtle when he saw her was, "I called Pastor Lindquist. He said he would start the prayer chain at the church for Anne." Howard felt relieved when he knew the friends on Cape Cod were beginning to pray. That was Anne's parents' home church in West Yarmouth, Massachusetts. They had known her since she was a girl and loved her dearly.

Driving to the hospital from the airport, Myrtle warned Albert, "When you see Anne, don't show your surprise or any fright on your face. Encourage her as much as you can. That's what the doctors say will help her the most." Anne was glad to see her father, but was suffering such pain and weakness that she could only manage a feeble smile as she reached out to grasp his hand and squeeze it ever so gently. He did not stay long—the tears had started to come and he did not want Anne to see him crying.

On returning from the hospital the three of them were very heavyhearted. They knelt together around the table in the kitchen and poured out their grief in loving prayers for Anne. God met them there and comforted them.

Later on Wednesday, Pastor Jones came to the Wetzell home to see Howard before making his daily call at the hospital. The two men talked and read a scripture together. Pastor Jones had something on his mind he wanted to say and was reluctant to leave. Stooping down to pick up some grass growing between the cobblestones in the front walk, he looked up with a very sober expression and said, "Howard, these blood things can be very serious, very serious." The solemnity of his voice penetrated Howard's consciousness like the thrust of a knife. Howard knew what he was trying to say—that Anne's condition was terribly grave.

That evening when Diane came home from school she begged to see her mother, so Howard took her down. But Anne was so critical she was allowed to stay only a few minutes. A friend, Alexis Haddix, was stopped in the corridor and not permitted to go in. Seeing Howard and Diane leaving Anne's room with Diane weeping, Alexis offered to take Diane home. With comforting companionship she went, leaving her father at the hospital. For the next several days no one was allowed to see Anne except Howard and Myrtle and her good friend, Kay Kramm. All phone calls were taken by the special nurse.

At this time the doctors thought that perhaps Anne's body was reacting to medication, but the fact was that she was taking very little medication. She was hemorrhaging so badly the doctors ordered that she be given cortizone and platelet packages. This was, of course, to supply the platelets she so desperately needed in her blood. (Platelets are small, flexible blobs of cellular material called cytoplasm. They help repair small blood vessels so blood does not leak out. Platelets gather at the point where skin is cut and blood vessels are severed to help seal the vessels. Certain substances in platelets are important to start the clotting process. They are measured according to how many are in each cubic millimeter of blood. Normal count is about 200,000 platelets in each cubic millimeter of blood.)

On Wednesday when the packages of platelets were administered Anne reacted violently, shaking all over. She went immediately into shock. She was cold and chilly and could feel herself fading away. Later, she said she thought she was soon to be in the presence of her Lord.

Watching closely, the doctor called for benedryl and gave it intravenously. When Anne regained consciousness, she opened her eyes to see the intern standing at the foot of her bed. He was visibly moved when the medication he had given took effect and brought her out of the coma. The tears in his eyes rolled down his cheeks.

Anne faced the reality that the Lord might be calling her home. Yet she wanted so much to live. She thought of her good, kind husband; how she loved him! Of Diane, so cherished, so much a part of her. She could not leave them, yet she knew she must be yielded to the will of God.

Howard was there by her side. He was beginning to show the strain of the uncertainty, the hourly vigil, the sleepless nights. He felt so helpless; yet he tried always to encourage Anne that she was going to get better. He leaned hard upon God.

Anne began to say something about her funeral. He could not let her talk like that. "Anne, please, don't talk about dying. You are going to get better. I know you are. It won't be long and you are going to get out of here. God is going to answer our prayers." He marveled as he listened to his own words that they could sound so hopeful.

But the bleeding continued. It was necessary to change Anne's dressing every half hour and the bed linens several times a day. The doctors were baffled. Her body was rejecting the blood she needed. Why?

That night at home Myrtle Eklund prayed more earnestly than ever before; not so much for healing as for the will of God. "Lord, she is in your hands. Whichever way it goes we will not be bitter because you make no mistakes. We will understand that you wanted to take her. Sometimes, Lord, when we pray we are a little bit selfish. Because we love her so much and she is the only one we have we want to keep her if it is possible. But above all else, dear Lord, we want your will to be done." Finally her heart rested in peace and submission.

Wednesday morning Pastor Jones called some of his parishioners and asked for special prayer for Anne. One of the women felt that a special time of prayer should be conducted at the church that day. She called several friends and at 3 o'clock they gathered around the altar at the little church on Brookes Avenue. Each of them prayed, placing trust in One who said, "Whatsoever ye shall ask in my name, that will I do, that the Father may be glorified in the Son" (John 14:13). God met them there and encouraged their faith; yet they realized that Anne's condition would call for continued prayer in the hours just ahead. Thus the network of prayer began to be enlarged as more people became involved in the burden for Anne's healing. God was moving in the hearts of his children to inspire faith for a miracle.

funeral arrangements: where it would be, who would preach the sermon, the songs to be sung, what she would wear. Her words came in brief sighs from her wasted body. Had she a premonition that this was the end? He dared not think about it. Life without Anne? It could not be. He marveled at the power he received to listen without bursting forth the tears he felt within him.

After Anne had talked a while she seemed to drift off a little. Howard left the room as Myrtle promised to call him if Anne awoke and asked for him. He found the public telephone near the elevators and made a call to Dr. Fred Ruymann (a baby hematologist) and a good Christian friend. His wife, Ann Ruymann, was the chairman of Christian Women's Clubs in the Washington area and a very good friend of Anne. Howard told Fred what was happening and described the treatment the doctors were giving Anne. Somehow he hoped that Fred could give him a spark of hope or perhaps think of something that could be done that the doctors were not doing. Fred replied, "That is the right treatment. I don't have any other recommendations. Howard, what would you like me to do?" He was kind and understanding; just talking to him gave Howard some relief. Howard replied, "Would you please call Anne's doctor and talk to him?"

Not knowing what to do and feeling very desperate at this point, Howard decided he would also call Dr. Reingold in the hope that possibly there had been some breakthrough in the case. When he learned that

Dr. Reingold was out of town, he was considerably shaken up. Speaking to Dr. Arnold Lear, his associate, he poured forth his desperate concern for Anne, his anxiety that all possible avenues of help be explored, and that every medical resource be utilized. There had to be an answer somewhere and he wanted them to do everything possible to look for that answer. Dr. Lear assured him they were doing all they could for Anne and had nothing new to report. After this Howard and Myrtle went home.

After Dr. Ruymann talked to Dr. Lear, the decision was made to transfer Anne to George Washington University Hospital a few blocks away. With Anne there, she could receive what further treatment might be necessary and be where the vital blood work was being done by the hematologists. Previously they had been reluctant to move her because she would have to go through the blood analysis all over again. The doctors were fearful that the procedure would be too much of a shock to her; they were not sure she could take it. The two phone calls evidently had caused the doctor to change his mind; some feel this move may have saved Anne's life.

When Howard entered the house, Albert said the hospital had been trying to reach him; Columbia Hospital wanted permission to take Anne to George Washington University Hospital. He returned the call immediately and gave his permission.

Fortunately Kay Kramm was at the hospital when the decision came to move Anne. Efficient person that

Perhaps there was still reason to hope. With this gleam of assurance Howard went back to the lobby to speak for a few minutes with his IBM friends. Some of these men had been in his home and were close friends, but he had never appreciated them before as he did that day when they left their jobs and drove all the way to George Washington University Hospital to show their sympathy for Anne and him. Howard realized again the truth that the difficult experiences of life not only bring out the best in us, but often help us to see anew the underlying good qualities of those about us. He prayed that he would not take for granted the friendship of men like these.

When Anne had arrived at the hospital that afternoon, she had been greeted by interns with needles to take more blood. Her veins were in a state of near collapse and it was difficult to get enough blood for the required tests. While they were gently probing her already battered body, the words of a lovely song broke into her cloudy consciousness:

I don't know about tomorrow
I just live from day to day;
I don't borrow from its sunshine,
For its skies may turn to gray;
I don't worry o'er the future,
For I know what Jesus said,
And today I'll walk beside Him
For He knows what is ahead.

Many things about tomorrow
I don't seem to understand;
But I know who holds tomorrow,
*And I know who holds my hand.**
—Ira Stanphill

Did she really have that kind of trust? Could she believe her Lord was holding her tomorrow in his hand? She had asked for his help. There was nothing else she could do and it seemed surely his hand was clasping hers even now. He was with her in the shadows.

**I Know Who Holds Tomorrow* by Ira Stanphill,

away, although he hated to ask them to leave the conference that meant so much to them.

The hotel clerk responded immediately; yes, Jim and Connie Armstrong were registered there and they would find them. They were just leaving the lobby to go to a healing service. When Howard told Jim the reason for his call—that Anne was critically ill and probably would not live—Jim said, "Let's pray," and there over the long-distance wires to Washington he sent up the most fervent, heartfelt prayer Howard had ever heard him utter. He was confident that prayer went straight to the throne of God and would get an answer.

Jim asked Howard, "What do you want me to do? Do you want us to come to Washington?"

Howard replied, his voice betraying his eagerness, "That's up to you; I know the conference means a lot to you. Perhaps it's too much to ask."

"No, we will be glad to come, Howard. I'll contact the others and we'll fly up right away."

"Okay," replied Howard, relieved. "If you want to come we will take care of the air ticket."

Ken and Connie Ekstrom were attending the Communion service in the large hotel auditorium and Jim went there to look for them. Since he could not pick them out of the more than two thousand people, he asked one of the officials to have an announcement made at the close of the Communion service, mentioning the nature of the emergency and asking Ken and Connie to meet him and his wife at the close of the service at the front of their hotel.

When Ken and Connie heard the announcement they knew it was serious. Since the healing service was next on the day's program, they made their way to the auditorium platform to see the leader who would be in charge. Their apparent anxiety and the urgency of the request brought Anne's need before the people for special prayer in that service.

Then they hurried to meet the Armstrongs. As they came into the lobby they met Ken Fraser, pastor of the Christian and Missionary Alliance Church in Pittsburg, Pennsylvania. They knew he was a tremendous prayer warrior, so they stopped long enough to mention Anne's need to him. He said, "Let's pray," and there, among the crowds mingling and pushing and hurrying to and fro, this man of God offered up an earnest prayer for Anne Wetzell's healing.

Meeting Jim and Connie, they discussed plans to go to Anne. They decided it would be best to call Howard and see what he would say. Should Jim go first and the rest follow later? While waiting for his answer they prayed and, despite the tremendous concern each felt, they also felt the peace of God and the assurance of Psalm 138:8, "The Lord will perfect that which concerneth thee."

Howard said, "Please come, all of you—now!"

A friend, Dick Jeuckstock, offered to drive them to the airport in Jim's car. Their hopes sank when the hotel attendant said the car could not leave the garage,

love me. I am so alone." Her voice quavered pitifully.

Howard and the pastor went over and talked to her about the love of Jesus. She listened very intently. Yes, she wanted to know his forgiving love. Would they pray for her? She reached out her hand as if for help. Howard took her hand and the pastor prayed first and then Howard. She had seemed unhappy and dissatisfied until then, but after that time of prayer she was calm and in the next hours seemed peaceful and at rest in her mind. Pastor Jones and Howard hoped fervently that she had accepted the Lord Jesus Christ into her heart. Anne felt if her hospital experience was instrumental in reaching this dear one with the love of God, it was worth it.

Later that morning Dr. Wilson came in and said they were taking Anne to X ray to see what was causing the hemorrhaging from the incision. She was still oozing blood from all over her body. Anne was too weak to pray. All she could think to say was, "Lord, touch me, please Lord, touch me." She knew others were praying, too, and felt their prayers.

It was a difficult day for Myrtle Eklund, Anne's mother. She had heard a friend just recently say that one of the hardest ordeals a parent must suffer is to give up an only child. Now she was facing that very situation. She did not know if she could bear it. But she kept her fears hidden and maintained poise and calm whenever she was by Anne's side.

When they came to get Anne for X rays the blood was literally spurting from the incision. Myrtle walked down to the little waiting room that had been a sanctuary to Howard and her all week. She broke some, then, being alone, and prayed for her only child.

Kay Kramm had come in that morning again. She had spent many, many long hours at the hospital that week and had found numerous opportunities to be a strong arm upon which Anne could lean. She went to X ray with Anne and when they came back she met Myrtle in the hall. Kay said, "You had better not go down there now—she is quite sick." Myrtle went again to her sanctuary to pray.

Later Dr. Wilson came to speak to Howard and Myrtle. He was a tall, slender man, wearing half-glasses, about forty-five years old, and very congenial. In his kind manner he said, "They wanted me to operate on her, but I'm not going to." At that point the doctors thought possibly the excessive bleeding from the incision was caused by a "bleeder" and they wanted him to go in and try to tie it off. His decision not to do this may have saved her life. Now they knew why the Lord had directed them to choose this particular Dr. Thomas A. Wilson when Anne was looking for a gynecologist weeks before!

Throughout the long hours of the day Anne did not improve, and gloom settled like a fog around those who waited and watched. One of the doctors told Howard that Anne was "in grave danger." Still, Howard spoke cheerfully and hopefully to Anne, keeping up her courage as well as his own. Knowing the Armstrongs and Ekstroms were arriving that evening gave him a mental lift each time he thought of them. When he told Anne they were coming, she smiled through the tears that came to her eyes and was glad. She did not remember asking for them.

Kay was sitting by the bed trying to help Anne with her noon meal when young Dr. Thompson, the intern, came down and said that Dr. Lear wanted to see her. Kay left the room, wondering what he wanted. She met him near the nurses' station. He walked up to her and said, "I think it would be best if you stayed around for the next couple of days; she isn't good."

Kay replied, "Do you mean she is worse?"

"It would be best if you didn't leave," he replied solemnly. "She does better when you are here. At times like this someone close to us is our greatest comfort."

Kay stood there without a word to say. As she turned and walked back to Anne's room she was humbly grateful that the Lord had given her a place to fill at this critical time in the life of her dear friend; grateful that friendship could mean sharing pain as well as pleasure.

Kay and Anne read many favorite passages from the Bible that week in their hours together. After this short talk with Dr. Lear, Kay read Psalm 56:13, "For thou hast delivered my soul from death; wilt not thou deliver my feet from falling, that I may walk before God in the light of the living." How filled with meaning it was, especially for Kay, who knew that in the next few hours Anne's life would hang in the balance between life and death!

Pastor Jones had to leave the hospital at about six o'clock to take care of other pressing commitments. The Ekstroms and Armstrongs were due to arrive about 7:30. Howard went downstairs to wait. Myrtle was with Anne, who was then resting comfortably and seemed to be holding her own.

Howard took the opportunity to relax for a few minutes in the comfortable chair in the large lobby entrance. He closed his eyes. As he lifted his heart in prayer once more, he was keenly aware of the nearness of God and the Everlasting Arms supporting him.

When Howard looked again toward the door, he saw Jim and Connie Armstrong and Ken and Connie Ekstrom hurrying up the hospital steps. His face lighted. "She's holding her own," he said as he greeted them. The two girls wept tears of thanks at his words.

As they approached Anne's room Howard warned them, "Remember now, no tears when we go in." He was glad he had prepared Anne for their coming. For them to walk in unexpectedly upon her would have alarmed Anne and she would have guessed the seriousness of her condition.

They waited at the door while the doctors were giving her a platelets transfusion. As her body stiffened, she began to shake uncontrollably. The gravity of her condition gripped all four of them. When the transfusion was over and she had become more normal, they went in. Connie Ekstrom, a nurse by profession, was struck immediately by the thought that she was bleeding to death.

As best she could, Anne greeted them, her eyes pleading for their help. They talked some and Anne mentioned that she would soon be seeing Mom and Dad Wetzell and "Mormor" and "Gramma" Eklund (her grandparents) and spoke again of her funeral.

Jim Armstrong, minister and friend, brought her real comfort with his kind words and assurances of God's love for her and His healing power. He prayed with her, and in that mysterious way known to his children, God came feelingly near. His Spirit ministered strength to their weary hearts and gave peace. No one present in that room could doubt that God had his hand on the situation and would guide them through this dark valley.

After about an hour Howard and Jim Armstrong left with Mrs. Eklund. The two Connies and Ken stayed until 12:30 when the night nurse came on duty. They promised Anne they would see her at seven in the morning, kissed her, and walked slowly down the long, now-deserted corridor and out. Even in the darkness the stars were shining brightly.

Howard seemed unable to cast off the grim thought that Anne might not make it. He believed God could heal her but he did not know if he would. When he arrived home he turned to his Bible. As the stillness of the night settled around him, he pled with God to give him an answer; to let him know if he was going to heal her. His heart cried out for some assurance, something to lift the terrible burden he had been carrying. His Bible opened to Romans 9 and his eyes fell upon the

17th verse: "Even for this same purpose have I raised thee up, that I might show my power in thee, and that my name might be declared throughout all the earth."

His heart gave a leap . . . there was his answer. It had come directly from God; not because his eyes fell upon that verse but because at that same instant God had witnessed to his heart that this was His message for Howard in that particular moment. Howard knelt by the bed, buried his head in his hands, and wept with thanks and joy at the assurance God had given him. He knew God was able to do what he had promised, and Romans 9:17 was his promise for Anne. The burden lifted, light came, and soon the morning dawned.

Chapter 8

Faithful Father

It hurt Anne's father deeply that his only daughter was suffering so. He wanted to go to her and comfort her, but he could not; he knew he would break down when he saw her. Because he found it so difficult to conceal his deep feelings he had decided it best not to visit her. Anne understood, being by nature much like her father.

While Albert Eklund could not support Anne by long hours at the hospital, there was another way in which he played a significant role in Anne's life at this time.

While still a young man in Sweden, Albert had decided that he would come to America. He had lived with his grandmother, a godly Christian woman. He was not a Christian at that time and as he was preparing to leave his grandmother said to him, "Albert, I will pray for you as long as my lips can move." He knew that she would and this brought him comfort as he set sail for a new land.

One day, not long after arriving, he was going by a Salvation Army Mission in the southern part of Brockton, Massachusetts and heard some beautiful gospel music. He went in and listened. He liked what he heard. Gradually he became interested in the meetings, attended regularly, and was converted. In the joy of his new-found experience in Christ he wrote to his grandmother in Sweden and told her that her prayers had been answered. He received this reply: "Everything's all right. Now I can go home."

Early Thursday morning Howard and Myrtle rushed off to the hospital and Diane caught her school bus on the corner. Albert was alone in the house. He needed someone to talk to and remembered that Howard had said, "Call Dorothea Webber any time you need help. She's a close friend and a good neighbor." Her phone barely rang when she answered. "Mrs. Webber, I'm Anne's father. Would you mind coming over?"

Dorothea had met Mr. Eklund briefly once before but when she walked into the house that morning she experienced one of those miracles in human relationships. They were drawn to each other like a magnet to steel. Perhaps it was his accent and manner of talking. Yes, he reminded her of her German grandfather. They shared a heart concern for one who was very dear to both of them; and also, related in Christ, they could bear one another's burden.

That day was arranged by an unseen Hand. Dorothea listened while Mr. Eklund talked and when he wept she prayed silently. When comforting words came to her mind she spoke them quietly to him. Sometimes there was silence as they shared in the feelings that found no words. Yet, there were no moments that were really desperate and empty, for there was a blending of spirits and minds and hearts. Sometimes they prayed aloud, or read the Bible, or just let the tears flow. It all seemed to be so right, so "ordered by the Lord."

Dorothea and Albert shared many hours together in this manner while waiting for news of Anne.

After fixing Albert's lunch one day Dorothea said to him, "Wouldn't you like to go outside and walk around?" But she could not persuade him to go. He was afraid the telephone would ring, that Anne might need him. He wanted to be near.

One morning a call came from Howard that Anne's condition was worse. As Albert walked through the house, his heart crushed with its burden, the words of one of his favorite gospel songs, "Burdens Are Lifted at Calvary," began to sing in his heart. Dorothea stepped over to the piano in the family room just off the kitchen and began to play it softly. Then she sang and Albert sang with her. It was a different kind of singing than she had ever done before, because it was as if she, as well as Albert, was reaching out to grasp something; reaching out in faith for Anne's healing. It brought release and comfort to both of them, singing together in the Spirit that way. There were other favorites until both their hearts were satisfied.

When they had finished Albert got down on his knees by the sofa and began to weep, dedicating his life completely to the Lord. He said, quite brokenly, "Lord, I completely dedicate myself to you." Dorothea was on her knees, too. He said, "I just want to be completely sold out to the Lord. Please, Lord, help Anne Marie to know that I am doing this."

Rising, he went upstairs for a while, and Dorothea assumed he was resting. After about half an hour he came back down. He was composed and quieted. He said to her, "You know, it is like a vision I've had—Anne sitting up in bed as if she was really well again. I do believe she is going to get well." He seemed relaxed and happy after that. In a little while Howard and Mrs. Eklund drove in and Dorothea went home.

Chapter 9

Life In The Blood

On Saturday morning, May 15, Anne's condition seemed to drop to a new low, if that was possible. Hope was about gone for her recovery unless something very unusual took place. Anne was hemorrhaging much from the incision of the hysterectomy, had gross blood in the urinary catheter, had a huge hematoma (blood tumor) on the hip from an injection, and another on the thigh. At this point the doctors still did not know why she was rejecting the blood but were trying desperately to replace it as fast as she was losing it. The platelet count continued to fall in spite of all they were doing. That morning it stood at a dangerous low of 4,000.

Connie Ekstrom, a nurse by profession, was perhaps more aware than the other family members of the gravity of the situation. Her professional knowledge told her that Anne's hours were numbered. Yet that morning on rising and seeking the Lord in prayer, she claimed the promise, "The prayer of faith shall save the sick." Would faith triumph? Throughout the day she breathed her prayer to God, "Lord, increase our faith." She kept a vigil by Anne's side doing those little comforting duties that so aid the sick. Anne was grateful for the tender touch of her hands and rested in the knowledge that she was in the best of care.

The doctors decided that Anne's condition required a private room, so they moved her to a small room at the end of the hall at noon.

Howard decided to go down to the hospital cafeteria for a cup of coffee. Just outside the door he met Dr. Thompson, Anne's internist. He looked very serious as he greeted Howard.

"Mr. Wetzell, have you seen your wife this morning?"

"Yes, I have," Howard replied, weariness showing in his eyes and in his voice.

"Has anybody told you how serious it is—that Anne might not live?"

"Yes, I am aware of that."

"You know, I am not the doctor in charge now." The doctor's words were tense and a little sharp.

"I know," Howard answered, not knowing what he was driving at. "She does not seem to be responding to the treatment. Is it possible that there is something else that should be tried?" Howard's lips were drawn tightly as he searched the doctor's face for an encouraging response.

Dr. Thompson looked up, his professional mask for a moment dropped, and in a low tone of voice touched by deep human emotion he said, "At times like this I wish I had never studied medicine. You know I am concerned about Anne and I really want to see her get better."

Howard again asked the question, his blue eyes narrowed, his brow furrowed, "Is there something else that you doctors should be trying?"

The doctor looked annoyed and, in an attempt to hide his feelings, said abruptly, "You let us take care of the medical side and you go to some church and pray or do whatever it is you do in church."

He walked away and Howard got the impression that he was quite upset. It dawned on Howard then that the doctors, too, were sensing their helplessness in Anne's case. Perhaps in their own private way they were hoping that the Christian prayers that surrounded her would be able to do what they were not able to do.

When Howard returned to Anne's floor, several of the blood donors had arrived. They were asked to wait in the waiting room. Reverend James Jones came in and asked if he could see Anne for a few minutes. When he saw her he knew in his heart that if God did not touch her soon she would not live long. She lay so still, was so very sick. Words came with difficulty as he prayed a short prayer. Howard met him in the hall as he came out. He asked if he would go down to the waiting room and talk to the donors, giving them a Christian witness and offering a prayer for Anne.

Arriving in the waiting room, Pastor Jones was overwhelmed at the large crowd of people who had gathered to donate blood. Twenty-five people had responded to the call for ten donors! They were of different religious faiths and from many walks of life.

Pastor Jones introduced himself, and then shared with them the meaningful concept of the giving of blood for the New Testament Christian. Briefly he explained how blood is a symbol of life and hope; that Christ's blood was given so that men may be redeemed from sin and find new life in him. As they were giving their blood that day for Anne's physical life, Christ had given his blood freely that we might have *eternal* life. He concluded with a prayer, asking God's special help for Anne in her time of crucial need.

While Pastor Jones and the friends waited for further instructions, Howard counseled with the doctor. "You seem to be delaying. The people are here and waiting but nothing has happened. What are the plans now?"

"Mr. Wetzell, our plans are to remove the spleen." (This is often done when platelets are being destroyed in the body.) For the first time Howard had understood what they were going to do, and that this was the reason for asking for the ten blood donors.

Apprehension stole into his heart again—he felt cold inside. "What are Anne's chances of pulling through that kind of an operation?"

The doctor replied soberly, "Not very good."

Howard, keeping as calm as he could, asked quietly, "What are her chances if she doesn't have an operation?"

Thoughtfully the doctor replied, "Perhaps, Mr. Wetzell, they would be better."

Howard was aware that although the doctor had not directly asked his permission to operate, he appeared to be looking for some direction. Howard said, "There is no question then of what you are going to do, if there is a chance that she would be better off without the operation."

There was a long moment of silence as the two men who held Anne's life in their hands contemplated the weight of that decision.

Finally the doctor looked at Howard with a trace of relief in his voice and said forthrightly, "Let's wait on the operation." Then he added as an afterthought, and his admiration came through, "You are a good man, Mr. Wetzell." The doctor went back into Anne's room and Howard went back to the waiting donors.

In that hushed little room he informed the donors that the doctor had now changed his mind and that, at least for the moment, their blood would not be needed. He apologized for any inconvenience they had been caused and thanked them for their willingness to come. He wondered, as did the pastor in later reflections, if somehow God had brought all of these people together to hear those impromptu words about the blood of Jesus Christ during that little session in the waiting room. Only eternity would tell.

Anne's condition remained unchanged throughout the day. There was some consolation that it had not worsened. That evening as Howard, Albert, Myrtle,

Connie, Ken, Jim, and Connie prayed around the table at supper, they were thankful for two things; that Anne was no worse and that the operation had been postponed. They believed God had miraculously intervened at the last moment to prevent it. Connie Ekstrom, at least, was convinced that if she had had the operation Anne would have died that day.

Later, Ken and Howard were to take Jim and Connie Armstrong to the airport for a ten o'clock flight to Buffalo. Connie Ekstrom decided to go back to the hospital to spend a few hours with Anne. The night hours brought a hush over the hospital rooms as one by one patients were put to bed and lights turned low. Sitting beside Anne's bed, Connie had a sense of the solemnities of life. We are born to die; life is brief; life is uncertain; circumstances are controlled by a power beyond us; we are objects of his mercy; all things are held in the hands of a loving Father. She felt an awesome nearness of the Spirit of God and knew that Anne's life was in his keeping. Even now he could take her or allow her to live. In her heart she believed that God would do what he knew was best and with that she was satisfied. Perhaps tomorrow they would know what he would do.

Chapter 10

Diane, Dorothea, Dolly, and Daniel

Along with his great concern for Anne, Howard began to be troubled about Diane, the beautiful daughter who was bearing this suffering with him so bravely. What was she feeling? How was she taking it? He prayed that his faith in God would be so strong that in the crisis he would be able to assure her. But as he prayed compassion and love seemed to flood his heart. If Anne should go, Diane would be all he had left. He remembered an earlier day when he had lost his own father and mother.

Diane had committed her life to Christ back in Endicott, New York when she was only a child. It was a day Howard would never forget. With joy, he and Anne had watched her learn to walk in the Christian way as they talked about Jesus in their home. From the example set before her Diane came to have her own private talks with God. Certainly this personal relationship with him would support her whatever the circumstances of life might bring. He longed to comfort her, to be near her, but his heart kept him with Anne every possible moment. Besides, Dorothea Webber, their good neighbor and friend in Flower Valley, had promised to look after Diane. Anne's condition had worsened and Dorothea had strengthened her motherly touch.

On Thursday of that week Dorothea picked Diane up at Magruder High School, along with Dolly, her own daughter. She was to take Dolly to Gaithersburg for her music lesson. When Diane got into the car, she looked at Dorothea, her eyes questioning and hopeful. "How is my mother?"

Dorothea knew at that time that Anne was very critical but she did not wish to alarm Diane. Since she did not wish to tell an untruth, she made a rather bland, noncommittal answer. Diane saw through Dorothea's attempt to conceal her knowledge of Anne's condition and her face dropped with disappointment as she looked out of the window without saying anything. As they drove the seven miles of winding country road toward Gaithersburg, she kept her composure and was quite calm. She ate supper with them that evening and Dorothea marveled at the stability of one so young.

Late Friday afternoon Howard called Dorothea and told her that Anne might not live through the night. His voice sounded so sad, so tired, so hopeless. Her heart ached for him. He asked her if Diane could stay at her home that night "in case the end comes." Dorothea assured him she would look after Diane and she and the family would be praying.

A tired, sober Diane walked to the Webber's home when school was out. For supper Dorothea served her favorite—spaghetti, salad, and chocolate cake. Joel and Dolly, Dorothea's teen-agers, had an appointment to keep and rushed off as soon as the meal was over. But Daniel, just turned twelve, proved to be the comfort Diane needed. He had a knack for saying and doing crazy things. Before long the two of them were 'turned on' to an evening of light banter and games that worked like magic. Sleep came quickly to Diane in the neighbor's hospitable home.

Next morning she went home for a few hours to be hostess to Reverend and Mrs. Jim Armstrong. Saturday evening she went with a group of teens to see *The Cross and the Switchblade,* arriving home rather early.

About 9:30 P.M. Dorothea's phone rang. It was Diane, but a terribly upset Diane. She was at home with her grandfather while the others were still at the hospital. Her words were so blurred with weeping no one could understand what she said. Over the sobbing Dorothea could hear the grandfather trying to console her, "Diane, don't take it so hard."

In minutes Dorothea was by her side. While she knew her mother was very ill, she had not expected to hear that she was dying. It was too hard to bear. If God should take her mother away she would not have anyone to go to. It would be so hard for her and her daddy. She realized anew how much she loved her precious mother, and even at sixteen, how very much she needed her.

Dorothea, Dolly, and Diane got down on their knees. Brokenhearted, Diane cried out, "God, you know I want my mother to get better. Please make her well, God . . ." Dolly, usually not given to tears, wept compassionately beside her friend and joined her in prayer. Dorothea felt the need of praying for Diane as well as for Anne. It had been a difficult week. Uncertainty, fear of the unknown, dread of the worst, had piled up a load as big as a mountain and the young heart of Diane gave way under its weight. While they were praying the sweetness of the love of God came to surround them and they seemed to be enfolded in his comforting Presence.

Soon Connie, Jim, Myrtle, and Howard came home. As soon as Howard saw Diane he knew she had been crying. "What's the matter, honey?" She broke into tears again. Tenderly Howard placed his arm around her shaking shoulders and they walked upstairs. There in the sanctuary of her room they shared their heartaches and hurts together.

Chapter 11

Promises and Patience

Sunday morning, May 16, dawned bright and beautiful. Connie reached for her Bible on the night stand as she awoke and turned to Psalm 37. Her eyes fell on verse 7, "Wait patiently for the Lord." She thought, How impatient we mortals are. How we want to hurry God to do what we think he should do! She determined in her heart to trust him for this day and wait patiently for the Lord.

On their 6:30 A.M. journey in Ken's car to the hospital, Howard turned the radio on. The familiar strains of Bill Gaither's "He Touched Me" filled the air. How appropriate seemed the words to Howard and Connie as they listened.

Shackled by a heavy burden,
'Neath a load of guilt and shame;
Then the hand of Jesus touched me,
And now I am no longer the same.

He touched me, Oh, He touched me,
And oh, the joy that floods my soul;

Something happened, and now I know,
*He touched me and made me whole.**

Their hearts were lifted and encouraged and faith was renewed. The morning indeed brought new hope for Anne. Upon arriving at the hospital they were surprised and elated to find that the hemorrhaging had definitely decreased and the bleeding from the hip had ceased to ooze. Anne looked encouraged.

Dr. Lear arrived shortly after Connie and Howard. He was pleased to see that the blood was beginning to clot. Connie ventured to ask him if it was all right for her to stay with Anne throughout the day, since she was a nurse. His advice was, "By all means, stay. They need you." Connie felt better then, and as the food trays were just arriving she helped Anne get ready for breakfast.

While Connie ministered to Anne she observed that the urinary output had sharply decreased. This could mean trouble, she thought . . . serious trouble. Alerted, the doctors called in a urologist and a very careful watch was focused on this new development.

While Connie and Howard were at the hospital, Ken had taken Diane and Dolly Webber to church in Gaithersburg. During the morning worship service Pastor Jones asked Ken for a word from Anne. Glad for the opportunity to speak of his faith, Ken came to the platform. He quoted Jeremiah 33:3 as the verse

*Copyright 1963 by William J. Gaither. All rights reserved. Used by permission.

he and the family were claiming for that day: "Call upon me, and I will answer thee, and show thee great and mighty things, which thou knowest not." He said he felt that the turning point in Anne's case was to be reached very soon. By faith they believed she would get well, though it would be a long way back for Anne to full recovery.

Howard and Connie spent the day with Anne; later Diane came down and saw her mother a few minutes with her Uncle Ken, along with Mrs. Eklund.

In his daily visit Pastor Jones read from Psalm 34, the same psalm Pastor Armstrong had read Friday night. . . . "I sought the Lord, and he heard me, and delivered me from all my fears. They looked unto him and were lightened; and their faces were not ashamed. This poor man cried, and the Lord heard him, and saved him out of all his troubles. . . . The eyes of the Lord are upon the righteous, and his ears are open unto their cry. . . . Many are the afflictions of the righteous; but the Lord delivereth him out of them all. . . . The Lord redeemeth the soul of his servants: and none of them that trust in him shall be desolate." What promises; what assurances of help! All who met around Anne's bedside that afternoon felt the power of God's Word giving them inner strength and faith for her recovery and restoration to health.

Connie and Ken left the hospital at four o'clock to get supper, returning to the hospital for a few minutes so that Ken could tell Anne good-bye before leaving for home by plane that evening. When he arrived at

National Airport in Washington, D.C. he had his tickets checked and found they had been made out wrong; they should be at Dulles Airport! That was more than a half-hour drive. They made a flying trip and had a few minutes to spare. As they entered the huge airport lobby, they saw two Vietnamese approaching and were surprised to recognize two young men they had met at the Council in Houston who had joined in prayer with them for Anne's healing! Their first words of greeting were, "How is she?" and "We've been praying for her." Connie briefly filled them in on Anne. They exchanged a few words and hurried on to the plane as their friends waved good-bye.

"How good the Lord is," said Connie, "to assure us again that many of his children are moving Heaven with their prayers."

Chapter 12

The Touch of Jesus

Sunday evening Howard sat alone in the hospital room with Anne. She had been too sick to eat any supper. Afterwards she was very tired and now seemed to be dozing. As he looked at her Howard noticed that her arms were swollen. Connie had seemed very worried about the fact that there was no output from the kidneys that day. Howard sensed that she had been trying to conceal how concerned she was. Anne turned restlessly and said to him weakly as she looked at her arms, "This is getting awfully tight."

The light was gone from her eyes. She seemed very weary from the long hours of fighting, so lifeless. Howard thought, This is the lowest she has been. She did not try to talk, to respond to what he said, to take any interest in what went on around her. Howard wondered wearily how much longer she would be able to hang on. Anne had always been a fighter. She loved life, enjoyed friends and family, and when she was well threw herself into each day's activities with zest and enthusiasm. How unlike her now! The hours dragged by. The night nurse came in and checked Anne and went solemnly out. Howard sat and silently prayed. After long hours he knew he must leave. He kissed her tenderly and left. Before getting the elevator down, he stopped briefly at the nurses' station and said to the night supervisor behind the desk, "Be sure to call me if there is any change."

Understandingly she nodded, "Of course, Mr. Wetzell."

Driving the parkway back home in the coolness of the spring night, he remembered again the promise God had given him on Friday evening! "For this same purpose have I raised thee up, that I might show my power in thee, and that my name might be declared throughout all the earth" (Romans 9:17). He clung to the promise and to the faithfulness of the God who made it. What comfort it brought him to repeat the words again and again as he journeyed homeward. He did not feel desperate nor panicky nor hopeless; he was simply aware that all was in the hands of the Almighty God and he knew whatever He did was best. In this trust his soul was at peace.

On Monday morning when Howard arrived he was told that while the hemorrhaging was much improved there had been no kidney output since midnight. Anne was scheduled to go to X ray at noon for an IVP Dye X-ray study which is given to see if the kidneys are functioning. At 11:30 Kay Kramm came in; Connie had come in earlier. When the doctors called for Anne to be taken to X ray, they found her so weak it took six interns to get her down to the X-ray complex. When she was gone, Kay and Connie went next door for lunch. Each had spent several hours of the night in prayer; each was looking up to God for strength for one more day.

Anne was weak but conscious while the interns worked over her, preparing her for the X rays. Anne tells of her experience in her own words:

"I lay quietly while they put the dye into my swollen body. My prayer was only a breath. 'Lord, Lord, you said you'd never give me any more than I could bear. I am just claiming this promise now.' The injection was so painful I couldn't hold back the tears. I cried out to the Lord to touch me there on that X-ray table. 'Lord, do you want to heal me? Is this your will?' At this point I knew I had to give up what I wanted and ask the Lord to do with me what he wanted. I must be ready to go or stay, to live or to die. 'Lord, I am willing, if you want to . . . take me. I'm ready to go. But, if you want to save my life, I give it to you . . . to glorify your Name.'

"The words of Bill Gaither's song came to me then, and I began in pitiful weak sounds to try to sing, 'He touched me, Oh, He touched me, and oh, the joy that floods my soul; something happened, and now I know, He touched me and made me whole.'

"I guess I was singing louder than I thought, for the X-ray technician came in and said, 'Were you saying something to me?'

"I said, 'No, I'm singing something to my Lord. I'm singing . . . "He Touched Me." Have you heard it?'

"She looked at me in a peculiar way and said, 'No, I've never heard that song.'

"The interns saw I was suffering painfully and one of them, Dr. Thompson, said, 'Would you like to have your two buddies here with you, Mrs. Wetzell?' I guess he knew how much it meant to me to have Kay and Connie standing by, and I said, 'Yes.' I knew, of course, that it was very unusual to allow anyone but the patient and technicians in the X-ray room, but Dr. Thompson, compassionate and understanding as he was, said, 'I'll see if I can find them.' "

At his request they went immediately to the X-ray room. Sensing how uncomfortable and cold Anne was, Connie got pillows, blankets, and even a water bottle for her feet.

The series of X rays was taken at intervals of fifteen to thirty minutes to see how the kidneys were functioning. Anne found the tedious experience more bearable with the comforts Connie had supplied. At one o'clock Kay reminded Anne that the Christian Women's Club Board was meeting at that hour and would be praying for her. From under her covers Anne whispered, "You know, I can feel their prayers, Kay." In her uncomfortable position there was that deep inner consciousness that she was being lifted to the throne of God in prayer by those friends who were concerned.

All was quiet. Connie and Kay were standing by her side, sometimes praying audibly, sometimes silently. Anne, eyes closed, was repeating snatches of the song "He Touched Me," pleading with God to touch her.

Suddenly, each of them heard the noise of a stream as the catheter started to drain. The fluid continued to come and increased its flow. The girls looked at each other and began to say, "Praise the Lord. He *has* touched her!" Anne began to sing with words they could all understand,

He touched me, Oh, He touched me,
And oh, the joy that floods my soul,
Something happened, and now I know,
*He touched me, and made me whole.**

Soon it was a trio of voices as Heaven came down and their hearts rejoiced. Then they laughed, hugged each other, and began to sing again,

Since I met this blessed Savior,
Since He cleansed and made me whole,
I will never cease to praise Him,
*I'll shout it while eternity rolls. . . .**

The intern and a doctor came running in. "What has happened?" Astonishment and bewildered looks covered their faces.

Then Kay pointed to the stream and said, "Look, her kidneys are functioning! It's still coming!" Other doctors and interns came in then, and all of them were trying to read the X rays. Connie hurried out and found a telephone down the hall to call Howard. "Praise the Lord!" he shouted back, "I'm coming right

---

down." Connie returned to X ray, where Anne lay smiling and happy. Kay was showing the doctors what God had done. The medical men were in some state of confusion and perplexity while Connie only bubbled and beamed.

At about 2:30 a very worried X-ray technician called Connie outside into the hall. She very bluntly said to Connie, "You have no business being so happy and encouraging Anne as you are. The X rays show that the kidneys have taken up none of the dye. The dye did not show up at all. It is very possible that the kidneys are *not* functioning. If this is true, Anne has only a few days to live. What you saw was only blood and dye coming out, not urine."

Connie felt for the moment that she might faint and reached for the wall to support herself. She had never realized before that it was such a long way "from the top of the mountain to the bottom of despair," as she said to Kay later.

Connie told it in these words: "While Anne was so very ill, she was very perceptive and never lost her keen awareness of what was going on around her. She could immediately pick up any worry or concern that anyone showed and I knew I could not look at her after talking to that technician until my composure returned. Fortunately, they were just about to take the last X ray. When Kay came out for that, I told her I had to talk with her. How glad I was that she was there! Kay went back in and told Anne we were going for coffee and would meet her back upstairs in her room.

"We picked up our coffee at the snack bar and found a corner in the back of the lunchroom where we could talk and not be disturbed. What would we do? Should we tell Howard? Could what the technician had said be true? If Anne had but a few days was it fair not to tell Howard and Mrs. Eklund? We prayed right there at the table, asking God for wisdom. We decided then that it would be best to ask one of the doctors. So Kay went back to Anne while I talked to Dr. Charles Thompson, Anne's internist.

"By this time he knew me pretty well. I asked him to level with me and to tell me just what he thought Anne's chances were. He said it was 'possible' that Anne's kidneys had been damaged and this was why they didn't show on X ray, but he said, 'Let's hope not,' and that in twenty-four to forty-eight hours they would know. I knew that Anne's BUN (blood test for kidney function) was well over 100, and normal was 20 to 40, and that she was becoming 'edematous'—a condition in which the body tissues retain an excessive amount of tissue fluid causing the body to swell. This was what Anne had realized when she had said to Howard, 'Look, my arms are swollen.'

"Dr. Thompson knew Howard had been sick about two months previously, so when I asked whether I should tell him he said, 'Why don't we wait a day or so and see if the kidneys do function.'

"I went back to Anne and Howard's home. I did not want to take away from their joy. I did not tell Howard and Mrs. Eklund what the technician had said to me nor reveal that I had spoken to Dr. Thompson. As soon as I could I went to my room.

"This was to be a night of spiritual warfare for me. I spent most of the night walking the floor and praying. I would pray and find faith taking hold and peace in my heart, and then the words of the X-ray technician would come flooding in and faith would falter. The verse came to me, 'Why are ye fearful, O ye of little faith?' (Matthew 8:26). I prayed again. So it went, a battle between fear and faith! Finally, at dawn a chorus came to my mind which I had not recalled for years, 'I Believe the Answer's on the Way.' Faith grasped the promise again, peace came, and I slept for about an hour."

Chapter 13

From Agony to Ecstasy

When Connie reached for her Bible on Tuesday morning, she turned to Jeremiah 33:3 and read again, "Call unto me, and I will answer thee, and show thee great and mighty things, which thou knowest not." It proved to be a prophetic scripture in more ways than Connie could imagine as she and Howard prepared to leave early for the hospital. Her main concern was that Anne's kidneys would function, for this was crucial.

However, she was hardly expecting the greeting they received as she and Howard approached the nurses' station. The nurse at the desk had such a happy smile when she saw them walking toward her that they felt sure there was good news. Yes, the kidneys had produced throughout the night in the surprising amount of 1750 cc.! God had answered! Evidently the kidneys were not damaged despite their fears to the contrary. It was a happy, smiling Anne that Howard embraced. And when Connie had given her a comforting pat, she began to sing, "He's the Christ of Every Crisis."

The doctors, who had looked so grim the day before, were now wearing smiles. The good news had spread around the floor and several new interns dropped in to confirm what they had heard. It looked like the crisis had been reached and Anne was out of danger, at least as far as her kidneys were concerned.

All of the doctors had been more than usually concerned with the reasons for Anne's very low platelet count. For days many of them had wrestled with this problem, discussing it with colleagues and talking it over during lunch and coffee breaks. They all pondered the baffling question: Why did Anne's body reject the platelets she so desperately needed?

A young black intern, Dr. Ray Nobil, was one of the many doctors who showed a great interest in Anne's case. He and some other interns were talking about her blood problem one day in the cafeteria. In a flash of inspiration he looked up from his sandwich and said, "Well, this might have us stumped here at GW, but I bet I know one man who could find the answer—Dr. Shulman at NIH. I wonder if he has been contacted? His field is platelets, and if anybody in the world can solve the problem, I think he's the one."

The other interns to whom he was talking concurred and wondered that no one had mentioned Dr. Shulman before. Why not ask Dr. Shulman?

On Tuesday morning they took a sample of Anne's blood as they had done regularly since she entered the hospital May 5. But this sample was to be sent to Dr. N. R. Shulman at the National Institutes of Health in Bethesda, Maryland, the noted specialist in blood platelets who has done considerable research in the field. His first report came back by phone: Anne's kidneys *were* functioning! The doctors were thrilled but could hardly believe it.

Connie stayed with Anne until after they had eaten lunch. She was desperately weary from lack of sleep and battling with doubts the night before. She called Kay, who came and relieved her watch.

The bleeding that had been continuous for the past week from so much of Anne's wretched body had now completely stopped. The frantic attempt to keep Anne in fresh linens was no longer necessary.

At the NIH lab in Bethesda Dr. Shulman was concerned with Anne's problem. Meticulously the technicians began their intensive search for the answer.

The nurse that evening was one of Anne's favorites. After supper Anne had occasion to speak to her at length about the answers to prayer that had come that day. Anne told her about the many friends who had been praying almost constantly. She told her about her kidneys beginning to function when they had stopped for several hours. The nurse replied, a little skeptically, "Sometimes the kidneys will stop when IVs are given."

"Yes, I know," said Anne, recalling some of her own nursing experiences. "But Someone had to start them again and that was my Savior."

The nurse looked down at the floor and simply said, "Yes." Looking up then, she asked, "But why did the hemorrhaging stop?" This seemed to be a greater wonder to her. Annie replied, "The doctors say they don't know why the hemorrhaging stopped, but I know.

It was God that did it! He touched me! He heard prayer and he stopped the bleeding. I know he was the one who did it!"

The heavy load he had carried was beginning to lift from Howard's shoulders. Hope and faith and joy gave him new feelings of exhilaration as he went about his daily routines. The tiredness was gone, his appetite returned, and he began to look for brighter days ahead.

Howard was by Anne's side on Wednesday morning. They read together the familiar promise of Philippians 4:6, "Be careful for nothing; but in every thing by prayer and supplication with thanksgiving let your requests be made known unto God," and also, James 5:16, "The effectual fervent prayer of a righteous man availeth much." Howard noted what a change had come over Anne. Her spirits were bright, her eyes were regaining their expression, and she was eager to talk about what God had done for her to any who came into the room.

That afternoon Dr. Lear came in with the report from Dr. Shulman's lab. He reduced the technical language of the report to layman's understanding by saying: "Anne's blood has a positive reaction to antibodies in platelets. After that one transfusion in 1958 with incompatible platelets Anne produced an isoantibody which attacked and destroyed her own platelets. However, this is self-limiting, and Anne's body will eventually reproduce and replace the platelets." So that was the answer! The doctor went on to tell them that Anne's case was very rare indeed, there being less than ten such cases in recorded medical history. (See *New England Journal of Medicine,* 1966, 275:5, Pages 243-248.)

Doctor Lear went on, "So, young lady, there is your answer. You are a very rare person indeed. You really had us baffled, and it is a miracle that you are alive today. Thanks to the work of Dr. Shulman and others we now know why you gave us all such a scare.

"Mrs. Wetzell, I'll insist that as soon as you are able you give some of your blood for storage so that, should you ever need a transfusion again, you would have some of your own blood available. You can never take a transfusion from anyone else again."

Howard turned eagerly toward Dr. Lear and asked the obvious question: "How did you happen to bring Dr. Shulman of NIH into this?"

Dr. Lear replied, "Well, it was Dr. Ray Nobil, the intern here, who put the pieces of the puzzle together. Everything necessary to find the answer is in Anne's medical history, but he is the one who hit upon the idea that perhaps the 1958 transfusion had sensitized her and she had built up antibodies and these caused the bad reaction to other transfusions. Of course Dr. Shulman's findings bore this out. Dr. Nobil has done something *very* noble!"

Later, when Dr. Nobil dropped in to see her, Anne asked him about his "discovery." He denied having done anything out of the ordinary and said, "It isn't just one doctor who does something like this. It is a team effort and it was all of us working together that finally brought the answer."

Anne replied, "Well, Dr. Nobil, I want to thank you for your part in bringing this about. God gives wisdom to men like you."

Tears rolled down the young doctor's face at her expression of gratitude, and he turned suddenly and walked out.

Now Anne had even more to share—God had not only stopped the flow of blood and returned the functioning of her kidneys to normal, he had also enabled the doctors to find the cause for her condition. The answers to prayer were coming so fast it was hard to keep up with them! Anne and her family hardly knew how to express the praise they felt. They knew God understood the thankfulness and gratitude in their hearts and simply let their joy overflow as best they could in their prayers and in testimony to those who came to see and listen.

That evening around the supper table there was great rejoicing. Mrs. Eklund sang "God Answers Prayer in the Morning" and they all joined in. There was laughter and there were tears of joy. The angels themselves could not have been happier.

Chapter 14

Those People Praying

On Thursday Dr. Thomas Wilson read Anne's chart as well as the report by Dr. Shulman. He came in to see her, smiling at what he had read and what he saw before his eyes.

"You know, Anne, we did everything to make you worse—everything, but you got better in spite of us."

Anne's face showed the inner joy and faith she felt. She was pretty that morning in her blue gown and bed jacket which Howard had brought her. "I told you, Dr. Wilson, that a lot of people were praying for me. God heard and answered their prayers. It's a miracle!"

"Yes," he said, "that was what must have done it. I am sure the Lord heard your friends' prayers."

Another doctor who had been on the case throughout and had been very disturbed by the adverse reaction of the blood transfusions said, "Mrs. Wetzell, when we were doing everything wrong, you got well anyway. It must have been the prayers of all those people."

Those praying people were indeed many. In Brockton, Massachusetts a church had a chain of prayer in which various concerned Christians were praying constantly day and night for Anne's recovery.

The wife of a cousin of Anne, Joan A., wrote, "We have had prayer meetings for you in many places: at the sink when I've been washing dishes, using the vacuum cleaner in all parts of the house, in the car after Wednesday night prayer meeting, after choir. . . . He has taught us all so much as we have been praying for you. Little Sarah continues to thank God each night for 'making Auntie Anne better.' "

Ted and Ken Kemp of Endwell, New York wrote to Anne, "We are filled with praise to our God and thankful to him for who he is, and what he continually does for us. We are rejoicing in the fact of his great hand ministering to your need. . . . Trust brings the 'afterwards' of God's blessing. Continue to look up—he is listening and caring. We pray daily that your progress continue. Great is our Lord and greatly to be praised . . ."

Miriam Armerding, wife of the president of Wheaton College, Wheaton, Illinois wrote: "Have been praying earnestly for you since I learned of your illness . . . Psalm 37:39-40 is a great comfort: 'But the salvation of the righteous is of the Lord: he is their strength in the time of trouble. And the Lord shall help them, and deliver them . . . because they trust in him.' "

Barbara L., a sister-in-law from Burlington, Massachusetts wrote: "Our thoughts and prayers are with you and for you constantly that God's healing hand be upon you according to his will. How wonderful it is when we can commit everything to him for he cares so much for each of us . . ."

A former Buddhist, Wonjunge, a member of Anne's Bible study group wrote, "I remember you in my prayer every day . . ."

Another friend in Anne's Bible study group, Karen E., wrote: "I am sure there is no one in that hospital receiving more prayers than you! It is almost like your condition is publicized on TV—that is how often we get word of you! My thoughts are with you almost constantly and often during the day I pray for your strength and that the doctors will have knowledge to help you. . . ."

From friends Ethel and Eldon N. in Brockton, Massachusetts came this note: "How much you have been in the thoughts and prayers of all your friends here and everywhere, and how we praise God for his marvelous grace, especially in times like these. After the frightening "low" time comes the great rejoicing when we see what our Lord can do . . ."

From another friend in Brockton, Bette H., was this message: "Anne, this has affected all of us who have known you and loved you. Our husbands have cried with us and we have prayed so diligently. It seems as though our minds were in constant prayer, and I know, for myself, how this experience has strengthened my own prayer life. We are so thankful you are on the road to recovery. We are still praying for you."

A friend, healed of cancer recently, Hulda H., wrote, "Isn't our Lord wonderful? We never cease to marvel at what he is able to do if we but ask and I know you, too, have experienced a miracle and are praising him. Sickness and sorrow come to us all, but through it we grow and learn how to share one another's burdens and cares. Life becomes more complete after overcoming defeat and our cups are filled to overflowing. May you continue to progress is my prayer . . ."

A friend from Anne's area Christian Women's Club, Dottie S., wrote, "You know we are holding you up in prayer each day. Our four boys, even little Joel, remember you. We think of you each day and want you to be assured that our contact for you with God is constant. His word to me for you today, Anne, is courage! I believe he has begun a great work in you. Let us stand on his great and mighty promise . . ."

It was indeed remarkable that so many different people in so many different places were praying for Anne unknown to each other. The unique way in which the Spirit of God laid this burden of prayer upon so many hearts was expressed in this writing from Eleanor C., a friend in Gaithersburg, Maryland:

"These days have been unlike any I have seen in a long time in our church. They have been days of much intercessory prayer by all who know Anne Wetzell.

"When the burden became too heavy I felt led to call my friend in California, Reverend Mrs. Doris McDowell, to ask her to pray also. She was attending a District Assembly in Pasadena at the time, and she requested prayer in that assembly for you. What a comfort to know those 500 or more saints were lifting you up in prayer.

"How wonderful at a time like this to feel that in Christ we are 'members one of another'; that we share our sorrows as well as our joys because we are of that great family of God where all are one in him. We are praising the Lord today for the good news that you are much improved, and we look forward to your full and complete recovery. . . ."

A Catholic neighbor, Sheila G., had anxiously followed Anne's condition daily. On Sunday, May 16, she had made a special request for prayer at St. Patrick's church in Flower Valley. When Howard came home on Monday he called her husband, Frank G., to tell him that Anne was better. When he asked where Sheila was, Frank replied, "She is over at the church." Howard walked over to the church and spotted her car on the parking lot. Stepping into St. Patrick's, he saw her kneeling in the pew and went over to whisper to her that Anne was better. She looked up in awe and said, "It's a miracle!" The mass was almost over at that time and so Howard also knelt in the pew for a few minutes. As they left the church, Sheila kept telling the people, "Anne Wetzell is better; Anne is going to live!" They also praised the Lord.

Later that day Howard went out to the Gaithersburg church and knelt with Pastor Jones at the altar to give thanks again for what God had done for Anne.

Howard works with Dr. Chawlow, who is a Ph.D. physicist, as well as a graduate of rabbinical school, an orthodox Jew and a rabbi. He called Howard on Saturday May 15 when Anne was so critically ill and assured him they would be praying. He mentioned then how the belief of fundamental Christians is in many ways similar to his Orthodox Judaism.

Other friends at IBM who worked with Howard said they had never seen so much concern among so many people for any one person.

Chapter 15

Witnesses to the Miracle

During the succeeding days Anne's body continued to put out large amounts of fluid, ridding the tissues of all the excess. Her daily output was now well over 3,000 cc., and her BUN was now down to 53. "I Believe in Miracles" became the exhilarating witness of the patient and others who were compelled to believe that God had wrought a special miracle.

She was still very weak, however, and was being fed intravenously. It was necessary for her to have special nurses from late afternoon to early morning. Finally, on Thursday when it was impossible to find a regular nurse for the three to eleven shift, Mrs. Eklund filled in.

The doctors were very careful about Anne's intake and output of fluids and prescribed a strict diet to get her electrolyte balance back. Each day they took tests to measure her potassium, sodium chloride, etc. Each day's chart showed progress to be slow but steady.

On Thursday, after the crisis was passed, Dr. Wilson came in again. He had not been in for several days, but was pleased with Anne's obvious improvement. With smiling eyes he looked to Anne, then Ken and Connie, who were visiting her.

"I don't know what you Christians are doing, nor how you 'do your thing,' but whatever it is, it seems to be working!"

Ken beamed and answered brightly, "We are not doing anything, doctor, but God is!"

Dr. Edward Adelson, a hematologist who was covering one day for Dr. Lear, visited Anne. He hadn't seen her for several days but the returning color of her skin brightened his hopes. "Say, young lady, you're really making improvement."

"Yes, isn't it just wonderful!" she replied joyfully. "God is giving me new strength moment by moment and how I praise him." There could be no mistake with the healing patient—the Almighty was doing wondrous things.

Dr. Adelson agreed, "Yes, we thank God first." He pointed upward and repeated, "He is first."

"You're so right, Doctor. But how I thank the Lord, too, for giving wisdom to medical men like you."

A young woman, Dr. Mary Colony, came in several nights when Anne was hemorrhaging so badly from the mouth. She kept close watch of Anne's blood condition and continued to make laboratory tests after her kidneys began to function again. As she left the room Anne would say, "I'll be praying." Dr. Colony knew her words meant, "I'm praying that test will show I'm improving!" With amusement Dr. Colony answered, "That seems to be our system; you pray while I go down to do the blood work." Later that evening when she returned with the report from the lab she said, "Our system seems to be working well; the report is good!"

Later, Pastor James Jones, in reflecting on the experience of Anne's healing, wrote:

"I cannot help but be impressed by the fact that this experience opened more doors of opportunity for sharing the good news than any other experience or event that I have known. Time and again in the hospital room with Anne's roommate and her family, in the waiting room, on the elevator, in the hallway, and other places I, as well as others who knew, had the opportunity to share something about this and give honor and glory to God."

Howard was quick to tell his co-workers at IBM what God had done. The church people of many faiths who had kept a prayer vigil shared the facts of Anne's healing with neighbors and friends. What God had done for one of his trusting children in the time of supreme testing became a tremendous stimulus to their faith.

On Thursday, Connie wrote, the Lord gave Anne and her the verse from Zechariah 4:6, "Not by power, nor by might, but by my spirit, saith the Lord." They were aware that they were beholding a work of the mighty God, something that he had wrought, not man. No wonder that Anne sang joyously, "Thank You, Jesus, for All You've Done."

It was an encouraging day when Anne was permitted to get out of bed to sit in the big chair by the window. For the first time since the onslaught of her illness she put her feet firmly on the floor.

Her friends, Robert and Althea Miller, who work among the Jewish people in Washington, D.C., found her sitting up and they rejoiced together. God had given them a promise for her from Romans 15:13, "Now the God of hope fill you with all joy and peace in believing, that ye may abound in hope, through the power of the Holy Ghost." Hope was the open door to all of them that afternoon.

A verse that Ken shared over the telephone with Connie when he heard the good news was, "The Spirit worketh miracles among you" (Galatians 3:5). How exciting to see prayer answered and a Spirit-wrought miracle. Their joy was expressed in a portion of Psalm 116 on Friday morning as Connie and Anne read together these words:

"I love the Lord, because he hath heard my voice and my supplications. Because he hath inclined his ear unto me, therefore will I call upon him as long as I live. The sorrows of death compassed me, and the pains of hell got hold upon me: I found trouble and sorrow. Then I called upon the name of the Lord. O Lord, I beseech thee, deliver my soul. Gracious is the Lord, and righteous; yea, our God is merciful. The Lord preserveth the simple: I was brought low, and he helped me.

"Return unto thy rest, O my soul; for the Lord hath dealt bountifully with thee. For thou hast delivered my soul from death, mine eyes from tears, and my feet from falling. I will walk before the Lord in the land of the living. I believed, therefore have I spoken: I was greatly afflicted: I said in my haste, All men are liars. What shall I render unto the Lord for all his benefits toward me? I will take the cup of salvation, and call upon the name of the Lord. I will pay my vows unto the Lord now in the presence of all his people."

Anne had promised God on the X-ray table that if he should allow her to live she would glorify him. This she endeavored to do by witnessing to all who came to see her and to all who spoke to her by telephone. The news spread rapidly and God's name was magnified. Through it all there was sweet awareness that they had experienced and witnessed an extraordinary demonstration of the love of God for one of his very needy children.

Chapter 16

To God Be the Glory

The doctors continued to be amazed at Anne's progress. On Friday, May 21, the intravenous feeding was discontinued and she was put on a regular hospital diet. She was even allowed to take a ride in the wheelchair down the hall. The next day will be remembered as the day Anne's case was presented in a paper by Dr. Charles Thompson to the George Washington University medical students. The rarity of her illness had been the talk of the entire hospital, and it was with interest that the students listened to the presentation. Many of them later dropped in to see Anne for themselves. She enjoyed talking with each of them as they came and could converse with them in a knowledgeable way because of her own medical background.

Also on that Saturday Dr. Nobil took blood from Mr. and Mrs. Eklund and from Diane to send to NIH to see if her rare type of blood had been inherited from parents or passed on to her daughter.

With returning health Anne remembered Diane's birthday. She would be sixteen on the 28th and that called for a celebration. With the help of her fine nurses it was arranged that Howard and Diane would take their evening meal with her. Dorothea Webber baked the birthday cake, wrapped it carefully, and sent it along in a box with Howard. Diane thought it the most beautiful cake she'd ever seen, pink and white with "Sixteen" engraved upon it.

Howard was handsome in his plaid Navy suit, and Diane—with her long, blond hair shining and wearing a light blue dress that matched her eyes—was radiant. Anne wore the new pink peignoir that her husband had given her. She was a weak but charming hostess, cutting the cake so that all the nurses and interns that dropped in could have a taste. It was a blessed, happy occasion.

Anne continued to lose fluid and lost thirteen pounds in two days. Her platelet count was now at 6,000 and climbing. Doctors assured her the count would continue upward though slowly at first. Anne was allowed to walk a little way down the hall with Ken and Connie by her side on Sunday.

That evening, just before Connie and Ken were to leave to return to their home in Brockton, they sat along with Howard and Anne's mother in Anne's room happily sharing the satisfaction of answered prayers. Ken picked up Anne's Bible from the stand and read Psalm 118:23-24:

"This is the Lord's doing; it is marvelous in our eyes. This is the day which the Lord hath made; we will rejoice and be glad in it."

"To God be the glory" was the deep feeling of their hearts. Anne, still showing black and blue splotches and still weak, had returned to much of her former cheerful self and joined in the happy spirit that filled the room.

Connie took the Bible from Ken and turned to Psalm 40:1 and 3:

"I waited patiently for the Lord; and he inclined unto me, and heard my cry. . . . He hath put a new song in my mouth, even praise unto our God: many shall see it, and fear, and shall trust in the Lord."

Then Howard said, "Let us pray." They bowed their heads while the words of thanks poured from his lips. "Lord, these verses from your Word express the feelings of all our hearts today. Accept our deepest thanks for what you have done for Anne. And let us from this day forward be able to tell to others the wonderful works of God. Amen."

Connie was quick to tell others, and took time to write to Kenneth C. Fraser, pastor of the Christian and Missionary Alliance Church in Pittsburgh, Pennsylvania who had prayed for Anne in the hotel lobby in Houston. Reverend Fraser said in his letter of reply to Connie and Ken:

"I read your letter with bated breath, and praised and magnified the Lord for he is 'a very present help in time of trouble.'

"Thank you for providing me with the details of the Divine intervention and healing. I have never heard of a case that parallels hers.

"One of my favorite verses of Scripture for an emergency like this is Psalm 55:18, 'He hath delivered my soul in peace from the battle that was against me: for there were many with me. . . .' "

It was a glorious, bright morning on June 6 that the doctors allowed Anne to go home, weeks sooner than she had expected. She promised that she would take it very easy and rest most of the time. The doctor warned her that she must be careful not to injure herself as she moved about. A bump any place on her body could cause severe bleeding. On several occasions she found after a warm handshake that her hand would be black and blue. Friends had to learn not to be too enthusiastic in their greeting in the days following.

The platelet count stood at 10,000 then, and in the next few weeks jumped to 25,000, then 140,000 and finally to 250,000 on August 6 when she went for her last examination. By the end of the summer Anne was back on her feet and assuming some of the routine activities of her normal life.

She continued to hear from her many friends who rejoiced with her in her healing experience. News of her recovery spread and she was asked to speak on numerous occasions, especially to women's groups, telling what God had done. Among the invitations was one to speak to a group of Christian State Department wives at the International Christian Leadership Fellowship House. This she was happy to do. She loved her Lord more than ever now and since she wanted to praise him at every opportunity, she spoke whenever she was invited to do so.

On January 31, 1972 Dr. Arnold Lear wrote the following letter to the American Red Cross instructing them to allow Anne to appear as her own donor so that her blood could be frozen and stored. The nature of her case is described in the following letter:

January 31, 1972

Dr. Evan Stone
American National Red Cross
Washington, D.C.

Dear Dr. Stone:

This note concerns Mrs. Anne Wetzell of Rockville, Maryland, whom we discussed on January 28, 1972. Mrs. Wetzell was admitted to the George Washington University Hospital in May of 1971, because of severe postoperative bleeding which after extensive studies, proved to be associated with post-transfusion purpura as a result of antibodies that had developed in response to prior blood transfusion or possible pregnancy problem some years ago. She had a rather severe course with excessive bleeding and associated renal shut down and extensive studies done while she was in the hospital in association with Dr. N. R. Shulman of the National Institutes of Health confirmed the specific identity of post-transfusion purpura.

She has gradually recovered from the anemia and the thrombocytopenia which had been present during that hospitalization in May and June of 1971, and as of most recent evaluation on January 25, patient was well, was not anemic and it was felt that now was the time to proceed with her serving as a donor for herself when and if the need for surgery and transfusion arises. Therefore, she is appearing here as a donor to have her blood frozen and stored, as we discussed, and will come in again on perhaps two more occasions over the next several months as her condition permits. If any additional data are required, please let me know.

Sincerely yours,

A. A. Lear, M.D.

Before her illness Anne often sang solos in her church. She had been asked to sing on Sunday morning, August 8, and while searching for the "right song" to express her overflowing gratitude for God's healing upon her body she ran across an old favorite of hers as well as her father's. These words of "Thanks to God" were penned many years ago but were perfect for Anne now:

Thanks to God for my Redeemer,
Thanks for all Thou dost provide,
Thanks for times now but a mem'ry,
Thanks for Jesus by my side!
Thanks for pleasant, balmy springtime,
Thanks for dark and dreary fall—
Thanks for tears by now forgotten,
Thanks for peace within my soul!
Thanks for prayers that Thou hast answered,
Thanks for what Thou dost deny!
Thanks for storms that I have weathered,
Thanks for all Thou dost supply!
Thanks for pain and thanks for pleasure,
Thanks for comfort in despair!
Thanks for grace that none can measure,
Thanks for love beyond compare!
Thanks for roses by the wayside,
Thanks for thorns their stems contain!

Thanks for home and thanks for fireside,
Thanks for hope, that sweet refrain!
Thanks for joy and thanks for sorrow,
Thanks for heav'nly peace with Thee!
Thanks for hope in the tomorrow,
*Thanks for all eternity.**

The beautiful lyrics set to the lovely Swedish melody became an anthem of exquisite praise to the Lord who hears the sufferer's cries. With great understanding and beauty the hymn writers had given Anne the words she needed to express her gratitude. The witness to his power flowed from this vessel over every worshiper present, as Anne's voice and presence testified to the miracle of his touch that brought her back from death to life.

---

*"Thanks to God" by C. E. Backstrum and J. A. Hultman, originally published by the Covenant Press, Chicago, Ill.

Breinigsville, PA USA
07 April 2010
235676BV00001B/21/P

9 781604 164954